ESSENTIAL
MANAGING
CREDIT

ADAM SHAW
AND
MARC ROBINSON

LONDON, NEW YORK, MUNICH,
MELBOURNE, DELHI

Project Editor Richard Gilbert
Senior Art Editor Sarah Cowley

DTP Designer Rajen Shah
Production Controller Sarah Sherlock

Managing Editor Adèle Hayward
Managing Art Editor Marianne Markham
Category Publisher Stephanie Jackson

Produced for Dorling Kindersley by
PORTAL PUBLISHING
43 Stanley Street, Brighton
East Sussex BN2 0GP

Creative Director Caroline Marklew
Editorial Director Lorraine Turner

First published in Great Britain in 2003
by Dorling Kindersley Limited,
80 Strand, London WC2R 0RL

A Penguin company

2 4 6 8 10 9 7 5 3 1

Copyright © 2003
Dorling Kindersley Limited, London

Text copyright © 2003
Adam Shaw and Marc Robinson

All rights reserved. No part of this publication
may be reproduced, stored in a retrieval
system, or transmitted in any form or by any
means, electronic, mechanical, photocopying,
recording, or otherwise, without the prior
permission of the copyright owner.

A CIP catalogue record for this book is available
from the British Library

ISBN 0 7513 3723 4

Reproduced by Colourscan, Singapore
Printed in Hong Kong by Wing King Tong

See our complete catalogue at
www.dk.com

CONTENTS

4 INTRODUCTION

EXPLORING THE CREDIT SYSTEM

6 UNDERSTANDING CREDIT

8 UNDERSTANDING HOW CREDIT WORKS

10 ANALYZING HOW THE CREDIT SYSTEM EVOLVED

OBTAINING CREDIT

12 APPLYING FOR CREDIT

14 REVIEWING THE CREDIT SYSTEM

16 REVIEWING YOUR CREDIT HISTORY

18 UNDERSTANDING CREDIT FILES

20 READING YOUR CREDIT FILE

Benefiting from Loans

- **22** Understanding Loans
- **24** Tailoring Loans to Suit Your Purposes
- **26** Choosing a Mortgage
- **28** Leveraging What You Have to Buy More
- **30** Using Secured Loans

Understanding Credit Cards

- **32** Choosing the Right Payment Plan
- **34** Analyzing Your Credit Card
- **36** Calculating the Cost of a Credit Card
- **38** Understanding Credit Card Statements
- **42** Calculating Charges
- **44** Exploring Card Benefits
- **46** Using Other Cards
- **48** Knowing Your Rights

Protecting Your Credit

- **50** Monitoring Your Credit File
- **52** Keeping Watch over Your Credit
- **54** Identifying Unfair Credit Practices

Managing Your Debt

- **56** Borrowing Wisely
- **58** Getting Help with Debt
- **60** Understanding Debt Collection Practices
- **62** Consolidating Debts
- **64** Handling Too Much Debt
- **66** Understanding Bankruptcy
- **68** Filing for Bankruptcy

- **70** Index
- **72** Acknowledgments

INTRODUCTION

Few aspects of personal finance play as important a role in our financial health as credit. Virtually every one of us uses it. Many people use it every day. Good credit can make our lives more convenient and organized. Poor credit can have the opposite effect. Managing Credit *is meant to give you the understanding to use credit wisely and to your best advantage. This book also presents guidelines for managing debt and dealing with the issues that arise when you are unable to repay what you borrow. Most of all, this book can help you build and maintain a good credit record, so you can have more of the things in life you might want but not otherwise be able to afford.*

Exploring the Credit System

If you understand what credit is and how it works, you will be well on your way to using it to your advantage.

Understanding Credit

Credit is intangible – you cannot touch, see, smell, taste, or hear it. Nevertheless, credit is something very valuable, yet fragile, because it is based on trust. It is a belief that others have that you can be trusted (or not) to keep your promise. If you have good credit, you are considered trustworthy. If you have bad credit, others may not trust you.

Using Credit for Leverage
You can buy things that you cannot pay for in cash by borrowing the money you need. For example, few people can pay cash for a home, but with credit they can buy a home that is otherwise unaffordable.

Borrowing for Convenience
You do not have to carry large sums of cash around with you to buy what you want, as long as someone is willing to trust your credit.

Budgeting for the Future
You can plan a budget and pay for things based on your future income. Knowing what you will be repaying each month makes planning easier.

UNDERSTANDING CREDIT

CHANGING LOOKS ▶
Like a chameleon, credit can take on different appearances.

IDENTIFYING FORMS OF CREDIT

Credit can be an opportunity as simple as a loan to pay for groceries (when you use your credit card at a supermarket), or as complex as buying a house (obtaining a mortgage). It can be:

- A loan where the money is paid to you, and you repay the bank.
- A loan that you repay gradually over time or repay in one lump sum at the end of an agreed term.
- A credit card, where you make purchases, the card issuer pays the merchant, and you repay the card issuer once a month.
- Other ways of paying for goods and services that do not actually require you to pay in full for the item when you receive it.

> **1** If you are credible, you are believable. A credible witness in court is one who is trustworthy.

GETTING A LOAN BASED ON CREDIT

Generally, anyone who can prove to a lender that the money loaned will be repaid on time and in full can get credit. In other words, anyone who can be trusted to keep that promise.

> **2** Credit is a bridge between you and the things you want to buy.

UNDERSTANDING HOW CREDIT WORKS

The credit world is a continuous cycle of borrowing and lending. To be able to keep the cycle going, everyone has to repay whatever sums are borrowed. Every borrower who repays on time allows the lender to repay the amount borrowed, which allows the lender's lender to do the same, and so on. When someone breaks the cycle, the entire system suffers.

APPROACHING A LENDER
People often want a product or service that costs more than they are willing or able to pay using their own cash. In these cases they may approach a lender, such as a credit card issuer or a bank, or ask the seller to arrange a loan for them.

BUYING ON CREDIT
People who sell things, such as shop owners, need to make sales to stay in business, so they are often willing to let you buy on credit. This allows sellers to make new sales and lenders to make new loans, so everyone can build their businesses.

SETTING THE BASE RATE
The base rate is the interest rate set by the Bank of England. When it rises, so do other rates such as mortgages. Lenders tend to charge more than the base rate.

RAISING FUNDS
Lenders make loans based on trust that their borrowers will repay faithfully. Their earnings come from the interest they charge. Once money is loaned, they may need to raise more cash to be able to make more loans. So lenders also borrow money from other lenders. As long as a lender's cost of borrowing is lower than the fee it charges for lending, it can make money, provided the sum borrowed is eventually repaid.

Understanding How Credit Works

Varying Rates of Interest

Interest rates can vary enormously between lenders. Some credit cards, for example, charge a lot more than others and there can be a huge difference between the best and the worst credit deals – so shop around for the lowest interest possible.

Identifying Money In All Its Different Forms

Not all the money we have is held in cash. In fact, the Bank of England says that only 3% of the total money supply is in notes and coins. The vast majority of the money is in the form of other instruments such as bank and building society deposits, credit card balances, loans, and bonds. As a credit society, we are generally less dependent on cash than we once were, and much more dependent on the credit system.

Making Loans to Organizations

People make loans to the Government every time they buy bonds, such as gilt-edged securities, otherwise known as "gilts". Gilts are thought to be among the safest of bonds because the Government is very unlikely to default on the loan. Since the risk is small, gilts often pay only a small amount of interest. Corporate bonds carry a greater risk of default because a company might go bankrupt. They are often given a risk rating, from AAA to junk bonds, and usually pay a higher interest rate in order to attract investors.

Understanding the Bank of England's Role

The Bank of England is the central bank for the United Kingdom. In 1997 it was given the freedom to set interest rates without political interference. The Bank's job is to control inflation by changing interest rates and thus control the cost of credit. It ensures that the financial system operates smoothly and tries to maintain the trust of the public. It is the banker to the banking system and manages the country's foreign exchange and gold reserves.

Controlling Inflation

The Monetary Policy Committee (MPC) sets base interest rates. It meets once a month to decide whether rates should be changed.

EXPLORING THE CREDIT SYSTEM

ANALYZING HOW THE CREDIT SYSTEM EVOLVED

The credit system evolved as lenders gave money to others in exchange for the promise of being repaid. Trial and error resulted in safeguards that reduced the lenders' risk and encouraged borrowers to repay their loans. This in turn created a larger pool of lenders to offer loans to borrowers like you. Here is a simplified version of how the system developed.

1. GETTING THE LOAN

You want to buy something but do not have the money. You ask to borrow someone else's money, promise to pay it back soon, and tell that person "you can trust me". The person says yes and becomes a lender. You borrow the money and pay it back whenever you feel like it. The lender realizes he or she received nothing of value in return for being without the money.

2. AGREEING TO PAY INTEREST

The next time you ask for a loan, the lender thinks, "What's in it for me?" The lender agrees to make the loan only if you pay back the money plus a little extra (*interest*). You say, "I promise to pay you back with a little extra. You can trust me to pay it back." You repay the money plus the interest, but you take a long time. The lender likes earning the little extra but is not happy about losing control of the money for an unpredictable amount of time.

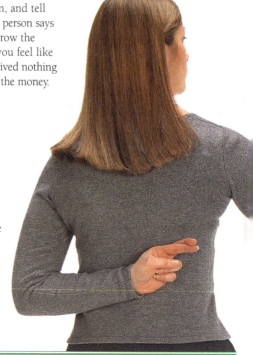

3. Promising to Pay by a Due Date

The next time you borrow money, the lender puts a time limit on the loan (a *due date*). You say, "I promise to repay you, plus a little extra, by a specific date." However, you repay later than promised. In the meantime, the lender had a chance to buy something, but lost the opportunity because you did not repay the money on time.

4. Arranging to Pay Higher Interest

The next time you ask for a loan, the lender hesitates. You have broken your promise and damaged the trust. The lender says that, since it is harder to trust you, the only way you can have another loan is if you pay more than "a little extra" (*higher interest*) by the due date. You agree. But what if you are late repaying again, or you never repay? The lender charged higher interest, but did not have either the interest or the money when it was needed. You have broken your promise again, and the lender has suffered again.

▼ **MAKING PROMISES**
Loaning money is a risk. To protect themselves, lenders add restrictions to guard against broken promises.

5. Providing Security for the Loan

You ask to borrow money one more time. The lender has two choices: (1) to say no, you are not worth the risk and you cannot be trusted, or (2) to say yes but also, since you cannot be trusted, to charge you a high interest rate and make you agree that if you do not repay on time, the lender can take some valuable property of yours and sell it to pay off the debt. Again you agree: if you break your promise, the lender can sell your property to collect the debt.

Now, if you do not repay the loan as promised, you could lose your property (an appliance, car, home, or even the money in your bank account). In short, breaking your promise will cost you more money and can put your property at risk. Now that you feel the risk, you may be more careful to fulfil your promise – and the lender may feel more secure.

OBTAINING CREDIT

Your credit is a reflection of you. It is a blend of your financial and personal qualities reviewed by lenders. A lender's offer of credit is an expression of trust in you that you will repay faithfully.

APPLYING FOR CREDIT

You ask for credit by completing an application. Here is the information you need to give the prospective lender.

ESTABLISHING TRUST

Part of trusting that you will repay what you borrow depends on your stability as a person and an income earner. For example, frequently moving home or changing jobs may indicate an unsettled, unreliable personality. It may also be a warning that the person could be hard to find should repayment become a problem. That is why many lenders ask you to list all of your addresses and employers over the last three or five years.

> **4** The application is the official way you ask for credit.

> **3** You commit a fraud if you lie on your credit application.

CONSIDERING RISK

Your credit profile does not make you a good or bad person, but it does make you a good or bad credit risk. Remember, though, that lenders want to give you credit because that is how they make money. They will say "no" only if they consider you too risky.

APPLYING FOR CREDIT

◀ **RAISING YOUR PROFILE**
Owning a home or having a fixed, permanent address will attest to your stability.

IDENTIFYING ASSETS

The things you own also yield insights. If you own a home, that demonstrates your stability. Shares and other investments show you can save money, and they may possibly be an emergency resource.

 Your application helps a lender decide if you are trustworthy.

ASSESSING DEBT

Have you taken out any other loans? How much do you already owe? How much credit has already been extended to you through credit cards and other lines of credit, even if you have not used it yet? In other words, are you now, or could you possibly ever become, *overextended* (owing more than you can afford to repay)?

STUDYING YOUR INCOME POTENTIAL

Your job history shows your earning potential: how much you have earned, whether there has been a steady increase, and what you earn now.

CALCULATING MONTHLY EXPENSES

Your essential living expenses, such as your rent or mortgage, electricity, water, and heating bills, are your current fixed *overhead costs*. The total amount of these costs is the minimum you can be expected to spend each month, excluding *discretionary spending* (money you spend any way you wish). This gives lenders a sense of the total amount your income will automatically be reduced by each month. They then estimate how much will be left to repay your loan.

Reviewing the Credit System

Once you get credit, here is what you do with it. It is a continuous cycle.

Accepting Credit

From utilities. When you ask for electricity or a telephone in your home, you enter the credit system. Suppliers of these services cannot know in advance how much electricity or telephone time you will use, so they let you use the products first and pay later.

From businesses. Businesses encourage you to buy on credit. You establish a relationship with them that makes it easier to sell things to you. When they send your statements, they can include new offers to you directly.

From mortgage lenders. A mortgage is usually the most important financial decision people make. It is also a long-term debt, often lasting for 25 years.

Buying on Credit

You buy from a merchant willing to trust your credit, and agree to pay the lender later. The lender pays the merchant. You can have what you want while you pay the lender for it.

OR

Storing Credit

You can save your credit for when you really need it. This is called having *buying power*. By storing your credit in this way, you can buy on the spur of the moment, beat a price increase, or take advantage of a sale.

REVIEWING THE CREDIT SYSTEM

6 Landlords' insurers may check your credit before they make you a firm offer of a tenancy.

7 A good credit history is a valuable asset and can greatly increase your buying power.

BUILDING CREDIBILITY

How you repay debt shows whether you can handle credit wisely. If you repay faithfully and handle any problems conscientiously, you will most likely be offered more credit. As you use credit, your ability to borrow will either increase or decrease, depending on how you lived up to your promise. It is your responsibility to see that your ability to repay matches your ability to borrow. Neglecting to make your payments and breaking your promise could make it difficult to get credit in the future and keep you from buying the things you want and need.

REPAYING YOUR DEBT

When you borrow money, you go into debt, and are required to repay what you borrow. You may or may not have to pay interest, depending upon the form of credit you use. Spreading payments over time will increase your cost of borrowing, because you will have to pay interest or other fees until you pay the money back. That is the cost of not having to pay cash when you buy something. It also allows you to budget and smooth out any anticipated rough periods.

THINGS TO KNOW

Here are ways you can use a credit card to build good credit:

- Use your card instead of writing cheques. Credit card transactions, unlike cheques, get recorded in your credit report.
- Pay your bill before the due date. This shows you are responsible and can be trusted, and it saves you finance charges.
- Use your card every month to make small purchases and pay off almost all, but not all, of the balance each month. However, although this method may build a slightly better credit rating, it will prove much more expensive in interest charges.

8 Building good credit means obtaining trust and keeping promises.

Reviewing Your Credit History

When you apply for credit, the lender checks on your credit history. This information first has to be gathered and put into a file. The file can be read only by properly accredited companies to determine whether you have a good or bad credit record. Where does this information come from?

Gathering Information

Details of your financial activities usually come from the following sources:

Businesses sending reports. Typically, any business that extends you credit sends out a monthly update on how well you are keeping up on your payments. In this way your credit rating is formed by the joint experience of a wide range of companies. It is an imperfect system, however. Some businesses send reports to only one of the credit reference agencies or do not send them regularly.

Public records. Any county court judgment (CCJ), bankruptcy, or individual voluntary agreement (IVA), as well as information from the electoral roll, will be added to your credit file.

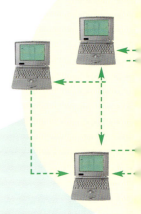

Using Agencies

There are three main credit reference agencies:
- Callcredit PLC, Consumer Services Team, PO Box 491, Leeds LS1 5XX
- Equifax, Credit File Advice Centre, PO Box 3001, Glasgow G81 2DT
- Experian, Consumer Help Service, PO Box 8000, Nottingham NG1 5GX

Reviewing Your Credit History

> **9** Any requests for your credit history will appear on the file.

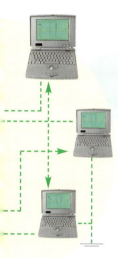

Recording County Court Judgments

If you have a county court judgment recorded against you, your credit file will show in which county court the CCJ was registered, and also the case number. It will not show who the plaintiff was – in other words, who was pursuing you for the unpaid debt. The best way to find out this information is to approach the county court. When you have identified the plaintiff, you should be able to get the plaintiff's contact details from the credit reference agency.

Obtaining Your Credit File

No one can see your file except an authorized organization. To gain access to a credit file, an organization must be registered with the Information Commissioner and the Office of Fair Trading.

Of course you can see your own file. To obtain a copy, you must write to the credit reference agencies and for a small fee they will send a copy to you. They will require the following information:

- Your full name, including title, forename, middle names, and surname (and maiden name if appropriate).
- Any other name you have been known by, if any.
- Your date of birth.
- Your current full address, including postcode.
- Any other addresses during the last six years.

> **10** A rejection of your application for credit may appear on a later credit file.

UNDERSTANDING CREDIT FILES

After they receive your application, lenders order a credit file on you in order to analyze your credit history. Typically, there are four categories of information in a credit file.

CHECKING PERSONAL INFORMATION

Your credit file will include a certain amount of personal information, such as your name, current and previous addresses, date of birth, spouse's name, number of dependants, and employment information. This information may not seem worth reviewing, but you should check it carefully. All of this data combines to verify that the person in the file is actually you, and prevents files becoming confused between two people who have similar national insurance numbers or who share the same surname.

INFORMING LENDERS

The credit reference agencies do not compile or maintain blacklists. They simply provide all the information they have collected about you in order to help lenders make an informed decision whether to accept or reject an application for credit. Even if you have been refused credit by one lender, another may accept you.

REVIEWING YOUR CREDIT HISTORY

Your credit history records how well you have kept your promises to lenders. It includes all current loans and many past loans, and lists account numbers, lenders' names, amounts borrowed, amounts of final payments, any amounts still owed or the credit limits, and the timeliness of payments. A late payment is a mark against you. If a collection agency has been used, it is also a mark against you, even if listed as "paid".

UNDERSTANDING CREDIT FILES

BEING PREPARED

The time to check your credit file is before you apply for credit. It is better than waiting for surprises and discovering that you have already been denied the loan.

11 Lenders use your past actions to decide whether a loan to you is worth the risk.

IDENTIFYING DISPUTES

Prospective lenders want to know if you have been in any disputes that have been serious enough to include the courts. These include county court judgments, any other actions for unpaid debts, and bankruptcy. Any of these are negatives, even if they have been paid, because actions of this kind may indicate future troubles for the lender.

MAKING ENQUIRIES

Every time someone asks to see a credit file, the search request is recorded. In other words, it leaves a footprint. These footprints help lenders ascertain how often a person has applied for credit or been investigated by a lender. Generally they will not see which organization has previously requested information, although they will know what type of credit was involved. For example, they will know whether it was in connection with a credit card, car loan, or mortgage. You may therefore be able to ask the credit reference agency to supply a list of those who have recently searched your file. No such footprint is left when you request a copy of your own file.

12 Errors can appear on credit files, so it is worth checking your own credit file.

HOW LONG CAN INFORMATION STAY ON A CREDIT FILE?

The Data Protection Act guidelines, drawn up between the credit reference agencies, state how long negative information is allowed to remain on your file:
- Lender searches: one or two years, depending on the agency.
- Defaults on loans: six years.
- County court judgments: six years.
- Bankruptcy: six years.

OBTAINING CREDIT

READING YOUR CREDIT FILE

The information on these two pages gives you a head start towards understanding your credit file and explains what to do about correcting errors and dealing with any negative items.

CHECKING YOUR FILE

When you receive a copy of your credit file, check it thoroughly. If you think that there is no basis for an entry, you can write to the credit reference agency and ask for it to be removed. If an entry is incorrect, you can ask for it to be removed or amended, stating why you think the entry is incorrect. The agency should respond within 28 days of receiving your letter. If the entry has been amended, the agency will send a copy to you.

13 Files from different agencies may look different, but the kinds of information should be the same.

DEALING WITH NEGATIVE ITEMS ON YOUR FILE

There are several ways you can deal with negative items on your credit file:
- Pay off any balances and ask the creditor to update your records.
- Wait for the information to be taken off your credit file.
- Write an explanation of the debt and ask the credit agency to add it to your file. This can be effective when dealing with debts that are the result of economic hardship or unemployment. The negative item will not be removed, but future creditors may take your explanation into consideration.

READING YOUR CREDIT FILE

SAMPLE CREDIT FILE

Electoral Roll Information
This confirms that you are registered at the address you have given when you apply for credit and how long you have lived there.

ELECTORAL ROLL INFORMATION
At: 1 New Avenue, Anytown, AB1 2CD
Smith, John	92 – 03
Smith, Margaret	92 – 03
Jones, Paul	90 – 91

Search Information
This shows enquiries made on your name in the last two years. The system is being changed so that only information relating to you is displayed.

SEARCH INFORMATION
At: 1 New Avenue, Anytown, AB1 2CD
Record Date:	12/01/03
Search Type:	Credit Enquiry
Client Name:	ACME Personal Finance
1st Applicant Details:	
Name:	Mr. John Smith
2nd Applicant Details	
Name:	Mrs. Margaret Smith

Court Information
This section lists details of any County Court Judgments (CCJs) and bankruptcies.

COURT INFORMATION
At: 1 New Avenue, Anytown, AB1 2CD
Court Date:	30/05/01
Case Number:	0001234
Court Name:	Anytown
Judgment Value:	£555.00
Defendant:	Mr. John Smith
Satisfied:	15/07/02

Insight Information
This information is provided monthly by lenders. It shows the commitments you already have and whether your payments are being paid on time.

INSIGHT INFORMATION
At: 1 New Avenue, Anytown, AB1 2CD
ACME Credit Card	Mrs. Margaret Smith	
Terms:	Monthly	
Balances:	Limit:	£1,500
	Outstanding:	£150.25
	Written off:	£00.00
Effective Dates:	Start:	02/12/02
	End:	
Monthly Status:	000000000000000	
Insight Last Updated:	05/02/03	

Monthly Status
This shows the status of monthly payments. The row of zeros indicates that payments have been received on time.

Insight Last Update
This shows the last time this information was updated.

Outstanding
This is the remaining amount due on the loan at the time the report was sent.

Benefiting from Loans

If a lender is willing to trust you, you will get a loan. The loan may come in the form of money, an authorization card, or the ability to borrow at your convenience.

Understanding Loans

Although different kinds of loans have different terms, they usually fall into one of four categories. You can pinpoint them using the following methods.

Assessing What You Can Borrow

The amount you borrow is called the *principal*. With some loans, you borrow it all at once. With others, you have a line of credit that lets you borrow up to a credit limit at any time.

With credit cards, for example, any principal you repay immediately becomes available to be borrowed again, as long as your credit remains in good standing. This agreement to let you borrow, repay, and borrow again is called *revolving credit*. As long as you continue to repay your debts, you should be able to borrow again.

Calculating Costs

Every loan has a cost. Although fees vary from loan to loan, the most common cost is interest. In most cases, the repayments you make are split. Part of each repayment goes to repay the amount you borrowed, and part goes to pay the interest.

There may be other fees. For example, some card issuers charge an annual fee, but they may waive it as a special promotion. Likewise, mortgage lenders often charge up-front fees for administration, performing valuations on properties to be purchased, and other work involved in setting up the loan. Read the small print before signing anything.

UNDERSTANDING LOANS

14 Good credit gives you the ability to get a loan when you need it.

15 In any loan document, the words "amount financed" simply mean the amount to be borrowed.

CHOOSING A PAYMENT PLAN

A payment plan has three parts.
How much. Each loan will be for a set amount or will be authorized up to a specified limit. The interest rate may be fixed so that your repayments stay the same. Alternatively, some loans are variable, which means the interest rate and repayments can go up and down. Others are capped: they are variable but cannot rise above a specified limit.
How often. Every loan must be paid back on a regular, scheduled basis. Most loans require you to make monthly repayments.
How long. A loan may be for any time period set by the lender.

FAILING TO REPAY: WHAT HAPPENS

Failing to repay on schedule can put you in *default*. Most lenders want to keep you as a customer, but polite reminders will become more serious requests if you do not pay. Some lenders may require that you put up some property you own as *collateral* (something they can take if you do not repay). This gives the lender some confidence that you will repay.

PROVIDING A GUARANTOR

A *guarantor* is a person who signs a mortgage agreement with the applicant. The guarantor is responsible for repaying the balance of the debt in the event that the applicant fails to repay the money.

BENEFITING FROM LOANS

TAILORING LOANS TO SUIT YOUR PURPOSES

Virtually anyone can lend you money, from relatives or employers to financial organizations. You can often get a better deal if you base your choice of lender on your reason for wanting the money.

BORROWING FOR A SPECIFIC PURPOSE

In some cases, lenders will extend credit only if you will use the money to further their business. The purpose of the loan – the sale of the product – is often more important than the loan itself.

Seller financing. Many department stores, retail chains, and car dealers offer loans to help them sell products. Two main types of loan are offered: credit deals and hire purchase. Under a credit deal, the customer buys the product immediately from the shop and becomes the owner of the product straight away. The customer has to pay back the loan under a separate agreement. Under a hire purchase arrangement, the customer does not own the product until he or she has made the final payment and then becomes the legal owner.

Special interest financing. Mortgage lenders do not sell homes directly, but they will lend money to people if it is used to buy a home. Since home loans are usually for large amounts, lenders require their borrowers to put up the property as security in case the loan is not repaid.

▲ **BUYING VEHICLES**
People with boat or car loans do not own their vehicles until the loan is fully repaid. Until that time, the lender is the owner.

Educational financing. Lenders of student loans insist that borrowers use their money for tuition costs and other education-related expenses. Since the borrower is buying an education, however, there is no tangible property for the person to pledge as security. The Government guarantees many student loans in order to encourage lenders to make funds available to borrowers, and protects them if a loan is not repaid.

TAILORING LOANS TO SUIT YOUR PURPOSES

EXTENDING CREDIT FOR ANY PURPOSE

Some lenders extend credit without requiring you to specify how you will use the money. Their first consideration is whether you are pledging an asset as security. The second thing they will consider is the quality of your credit rating. Finally, they may also take into account your purpose for the loan. Here are some examples.

Asset-based loan. A bank, building society, or insurance company may let you borrow against the value of your insurance, home, or investments if your assets have enough value. Typically, asset-based loans have lower interest rates than those of conventional loans. The lender reasons that if you own these assets, they are a testament to your financial responsibility and credibility. You are also protecting the lender by pledging assets of sufficient value to cover the loan in case you fail to make the repayments.

Line of credit. This type of loan is a very useful tool in today's world, although it is tempting to use it indiscriminately. When a lender offers you a line of credit, you are given a credit limit (a maximum amount you can borrow). You are then free to borrow up to that limit at any time for any purpose. Credit cards are the most common example of this type of loan, but home equity loans can also be used as lines of credit. Many banks are now offering lines of credit to customers.

Personal loan. You may get a loan on the strength of your credit history, or the lender may ask you to pledge an asset as security.

Pawning. Pawnbrokers lend money to people without checking their credit history. You simply offer an item of value, the broker lends you a small percentage of the item's value, and holds the item for an agreed period of time. You can pay off the loan within that time and reclaim the item. If you do not, the broker can sell it. Interest on these loans tends to be high. You may also have to pay for insurance and storage.

16 The best loan for your specific needs may come from a lender who specializes in loans for the purpose you have in mind.

BENEFITING FROM LOANS

CHOOSING A MORTGAGE

A mortgage is usually the biggest single debt anyone will ever have. Getting the wrong mortgage, or misunderstanding the type of mortgage you have, can be very serious and it is wise to take independent professional advice before committing yourself to anything.

UNDERSTANDING MORTGAGES

A mortgage is as important as the home you are going to buy with it, so do not spend all your time choosing the home without spending a considerable amount of time choosing the mortgage. A mortgage is just another form of debt. In essence it is a loan that is guaranteed by a property. If you cannot pay back your loan, the lender can force you to sell your home in order to get the money back.

DECIDING HOW MUCH TO BORROW

Typically you can borrow up to three-and-a-half times your income if you are buying on your own, or two-and-a-half times the joint income of you and your partner. The amount you can borrow also depends on the value of your home. Most lenders will allow you to borrow up to 95% of the value of a property, although it is possible to get a better deal if you borrow less and pay more yourself. The loan rate set by the lender is called the standard variable rate (SVR).

Always shop around and compare different mortgages in order to get the best deal possible.

BUYING A HOME WITHOUT A DEPOSIT

Some lenders will let you borrow 100% or more of a property's value, but these mortgages are more expensive. Also, you should make sure that you are not taking on too much debt.

CHOOSING A MORTGAGE

DEFINING THE MAIN TYPES OF MORTGAGE

There are two main types of mortgage: interest only and capital repayment. However, there are many variations on these two themes so you should make sure you understand exactly which type of mortgage you are being offered. Each borrower's needs are different, so consult an independent financial adviser.

OPTING FOR INTEREST ONLY

An interest-only mortgage allows you to repay just the interest on your loan, so you also need to take out an investment that will mature in time to pay off the original amount borrowed. If your investment performs well, you may have some money left over after paying back your mortgage. However, there is also a risk that the investment will underperform and leave you to make up any shortfall. The most popular investment for these mortgages used to be an endowment policy, but they have been hit by problems recently. Poor returns on the stock market mean endowments might not provide enough money to pay off the whole mortgage.

SELECTING THE REPAYMENT METHOD

With a repayment mortgage you pay back both the interest and loan capital so that, at the end of your mortgage period, there is no money owing. In the early years your repayments are mostly taken up by interest, so it might seem that the outstanding balance never gets lower, but over time the debt will decrease because more of your repayments will go towards paying off the capital owed rather than simply paying interest.

 18 Some lenders impose a penalty if you redeem part or all of your mortgage early, so check first.

GETTING A FIXED-RATE MORTGAGE

These may not be the most competitive mortgages, but they can offer peace of mind. Since the interest rate is fixed for a specified period of time, you know exactly what the mortgage will cost you.

LEVERAGING WHAT YOU HAVE TO BUY MORE

To a lender, the most attractive borrower is someone with proven financial responsibility or someone with assets under the lender's control. With these advantages, you can often get a loan more quickly and on better terms by leveraging the power of your assets.

RELEASING YOUR HOME'S EQUITY

One of the most tempting resources at your disposal is your home's equity (the difference between what you owe on your home and what the property is worth). Many lenders require you to have at least 30% equity. For example, if you own a home worth £100,000 you would owe no more than £70,000, leaving £30,000 – or 30% – as equity. In exchange for the loan, you will give the lender a *second charge*. Your original mortgage lender has the *first charge*. If you fail to make the payments on the equity loan, the lender can force the sale of the home, even if your other mortgage payments are on time. There are two main ways to borrow against your home's equity.

Second mortgages. These loans give you a lump sum that you repay in scheduled instalments.

Equity release schemes. These let you borrow money using your home as collateral. Some let you defer repaying until after your death, when the lender sells your home to recover the money.

USING SECURITIES TO BORROW MONEY

In the United States, a number of investors trade on what is called *margin*. This is not common in the United Kingdom, but the practice is growing. Brokerage firms effectively lend money on margin. This means that they will lend you money equal to a percentage of the value of the securities in your account. The firm gives you the loan, and you give the firm the right to sell your securities if you fail to repay. You pay interest on the loan and make payments in regular instalments.

The attraction of margin loans is the interest rate, which is often a few points less than you would pay at a bank. Margin loans can be risky, however. If the prices of your securities drop to a point where the securities' value does not cover the amount required to protect the brokerage firm, the firm will make a *margin call* (ask you to put in more money or pledge more securities). Failure to meet a margin call means an instant sale of the securities you have already pledged – even if at a loss.

UTILIZING YOUR LIFE INSURANCE

If you have a whole-of-life policy (not term insurance), you may be able to borrow an amount equal to its *cash surrender value*. This is the amount of cash you will receive if you stop paying premiums and surrender the policy. The more premiums you pay, the more the cash surrender value increases.

The interest charged on this kind of loan varies from company to company, but it is often lower than the interest charged on a bank loan. Also, an insurance company is not as concerned about being repaid. It will simply deduct what is owed before paying your beneficiaries the remaining value of the policy.

USING THE POWER OF LEVERAGING

In the financial world, leverage can help achieve otherwise impossible feats. It involves borrowing money to invest. If the profit is more than the interest, you have made money, but if the investment goes wrong, you have lost somebody else's money. Leverage deals can therefore be very risky. Leverage is also known as "gearing".

19 Better credit increases your chances of leveraging your assets for a loan.

Using Secured Loans

Some loans require security. A lender has to believe that you will repay what you borrow. If the risk is too great to trust your promise, you will have to agree to a secured loan. The lender requires you to pledge an item of value that can be sold if you do not repay the loan. Here is how it works.

Arranging the Exchange

In this arrangement, the lender gives you the loan and you give the lender the right to own a specific asset of yours if you fail to repay faithfully. If you are buying an expensive item on credit, such as a home, the home itself will be the secured asset. For other loans, a lender can ask for another item you own as security. It is up to you whether or not to agree to risk losing that item.

Tying Property to a Loan

When you tie an asset to a loan – in other words when you pledge the asset as security for part or all of a loan (called collateral) – you are giving up the right to sell it without the lender's written permission. If you deposit cash in an account as security, for example, you will not be permitted to withdraw that cash without the lender's permission. Once you have repaid the loan, however, the lender no longer has any right to your property.

Failing to Repay on Schedule

If you default on the loan the lender, by agreement, can find other ways to collect the debt. Some lenders may be lenient if you make late payments. Others will hold strictly to the terms of your agreement.

Repossessing the Property

If the property is an appliance or a car, the lender may hire someone to come and take it from you. If it is your home, the lender will have to apply to a court for a *repossession order*.

Identifying Reasons for Secured Loans

Secured loans are usually offered for one of two reasons: either the loan is for a large amount, such as for a car or a home, or your credit record shows you have not repaid loans on schedule.

Using Secured Loans

20 When lenders have a lot of money at stake, they may prefer a secured interest in order to protect their investment.

21 Always check that you can afford to repay a loan, especially if you are asked to pledge your home as security.

▼ SELLING YOUR PROPERTY
A lender may sell your property in order to recoup any money owed. If the sale does not raise enough to cover the debt, you will still have to pay the rest.

Selling off Repossessed Items

Your property may be sold at auction or as secondhand. If your home is repossessed, you will be forced to move out so the lender can either auction it or sell it to someone else. The lender will use the proceeds to pay off as much of your loan as possible. Any other lender with a security interest in the same property will take what it is owed. Afterwards you may still be left with a debt you owe the lender.

Things to Know

- Lenders who offer you a secured loan may not review your credit file as carefully as they would if they were giving you an unsecured loan. Since they can take something of value from you if you do not pay, they may focus more on how much cash, income, and debt you have.

- Joint credit is given based on the assets, income, and credit history of both applicants. They will both be responsible for the debt – even if they separate.

- If you have negative credit on your file it can be outweighed by positive information, especially if the negative item was small and occurred some time ago.

- If you still owe money after a lender takes your property, the debt will not go away – it becomes an unsecured debt. If you do not repay it voluntarily, the lender can try to ask a court to order you to do so. It is also possible that your wages will be *garnished*, meaning that some of each of your pay cheques will be paid to the lender instead of to you.

- Once a default is on your credit file, many lenders will refuse you new loans. Those who offer you credit will probably charge much higher interest rates to make their risk worthwhile. You may then have to begin rebuilding your credit history by applying for small, secured loans and repaying them faithfully.

Understanding Credit Cards

Nowadays credit cards are the most widely used form of credit. There is a credit card for almost everyone, each with its own fees, benefits, and other features.

Choosing the Right Payment Plan

To choose the right card, consider how you wish to repay the money you borrow. With a good credit record, the choice is yours.

Repaying In Full: Charge Cards

These cards show that you have been extended credit, but only for short periods of time. These are usually for 30 days, but can vary according to the terms set by the credit card issuer. Charge cards require you to pay in full by the due date for any item that appears on your statement. There are no interest charges as long as you settle in full in the time specified. If you pay late, you may be charged a fee for late payment in addition to interest.

Repaying Later: Credit Cards

Paying by credit card is a flexible form of borrowing. It is an open line of credit you can use and repay at your own pace, as long as you make the required minimum payment by the due date each month. You may pay interest on what you borrow, or you may be given a period of time to repay in full without interest. Credit cards allow you to borrow up to a preagreed limit, known as the *credit limit*. Any amount you repay is immediately available to borrow again, after deducting any interest charged. This is called revolving credit.

CHOOSING THE RIGHT PAYMENT PLAN

PAYING AS YOU GO: DEBIT CARDS

If you do not want to incur interest charges, cannot get credit, or simply do not like buying on credit, you can still have a convenient way to pay. You can use a debit card, which does not actually give you credit. Instead, when you use it, your bank takes (*debits*) the money from your current account and sends it directly to the merchant. Switch cards work like this. If the money is not in your account, the transaction will be rejected. ATM cards, which are used for banking at automated cash machines, are the most popular debit cards. However, these cards offer card issuers less protection against fraud than credit cards because it is difficult for them to recover money already paid from your account.

INCREASING DEBT

Credit card debt has increased rapidly since the early 1990s. Some of that is because of a rise in disposable income, but even the level of debt as a proportion of income has risen slightly. Cardholders in the UK now spend around £91 billion a year with their credit cards, which works out to £2,900 per second.

 22 A credit card will work like a charge card if you repay in full each month.

USING CREDIT CARDS

There are 55 million cards in circulation in the UK and the average British cardholder has two credit cards. About 60% of people pay off their debt each month without incurring interest. The average annual credit card spend is around £2,900 and there are around 1.6 billion credit card transactions in any one year. Credit card spending accounts for around 21% of high street spending.

PAYING BY ▶ CREDIT CARD
Credit cards provide a convenient way to pay, and are inexpensive as long as you repay in full and on time each month.

UNDERSTANDING CREDIT CARDS

ANALYZING YOUR CREDIT CARD

A credit card is an authorization card. It is proof that someone trusts you and has authorized you to buy on credit. Like a passport that allows you to travel, or a licence that tells police you are permitted to drive a car, this card authorizes you to buy a product without cash. The card issuer promises to pay the merchant. The issuer then expects to be repaid by you.

Valid from Date
This is the earliest date you can begin using the card.

Card Number
This number is embossed on the card, which makes an imprint possible and renders counterfeiting more difficult. Each card issuer has its own numbering formats. Many cards have the first four digits printed on the card below the embossed numbers as extra security. This prevents anyone from altering the embossed numbers. It may also have a security number printed somewhere else on the card, such as on the signature authorization strip.

Your Full Name
This is the name you should give when using your credit card to place orders by telephone or by other means. It is the name the card issuer uses to verify your identity when dealing with merchants.

Expiry Date
After this date the card will no longer be valid for use. A card is usually valid for one to three years. If you maintain a good credit record with the card issuer, you will automatically be sent a new card before your current one expires.

Hologram
Almost all cards now have a holographic image, which seems to move when you tip the card back and forth. The image is pressed on coloured foil and contains ink that is visible only under an ultraviolet lamp. Holograms protect cards from being counterfeited.

23 Keep your card away from magnets. They could potentially erase the data on the magnetic strip.

Analyzing Your Credit Card

Using Your PIN

A PIN is a Personal Identification Number, a password. To use your card for cash advances or withdrawals at an ATM, you will need to create a PIN. Protect your PIN very carefully. Do not write it down, tell it to anyone, put it on the card, or let anyone overhear you repeating it.

Shopping Around

There are more than 90 million payment cards currently in circulation in the UK. These payment cards make up a huge range of credit cards, debit cards, and store cards, and provide consumers with a bewildering number of ways to pay their bills. It is best to shop around to get the very best deals on offer.

Customer Service Number
For lost or stolen cards, or if you simply have questions about your account, call the number on the back of the card.

Authorized Signature Strip
You should sign the back of your card as soon as you receive it in the post. This protects you from anyone using your card should it become lost or stolen. Your signature is one way to prove you did not make purchases that are in dispute. The signature strip on most cards is tamper-resistant. If anyone tries to erase your signature and forge a different one onto your card, the strip will be destroyed, alerting merchants to the forgery.

Magnetic Strip
The black strip on the back of the card is magnetic so that it can interact with the electronic approval machines you see at most shops. The strip contains your name, credit limit, PIN, the expiry date, account number, and other data.

Transmitting Data Quickly

A credit card transaction between Japan and Hawaii takes less than a second to approve. The data travels at more than 4,464,456 kilometres an hour, 3,647 times the speed of sound.

24 New credit cards have smart chips in order to improve their security.

Understanding Credit Cards

Calculating the Cost of a Credit Card

Before you sign an agreement for a credit card, be sure you understand the basic costs you are accepting.

Interest Rates

Different cards come with different interest rates. The amount of the interest rate is quoted when you apply for your credit card, but it tends to change as interest rates rise and fall elsewhere in the economy. Generally, the interest rates charged by credit card issuers can be very high. Any interest rate should be clearly explained to you, and so should the length of any interest-free or discounted period.

Introductory rates. Many cards offer special introductory rates so that for the first few months the rate is unusually low. These offers can be very enticing, but remember that the interest rate will increase sharply once the introductory offer has ended. There is a growing band of people who move from one card to another, making use of a number of introductory rates, so that they continually pay a discounted fee. This practice can save money, but remember that many issuers who offer low introductory rates include a clause in the credit agreement stating that if you make a late payment, your rate can immediately adjust to the full rate.

25 The card issuer may raise your interest rate if you make a late payment.

26 Read the fine print on the inserts that come with your credit card. It may signal fee changes.

▼ **RAISING INTEREST**
Once the introductory rate has run out, the real cost of interest can increase sharply. Make sure you know when that will happen.

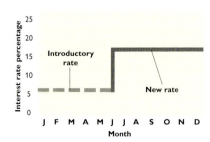

Analyzing Fees

Purchases. Interest is not usually charged on purchases if you pay for them in full by the due date.
Cash advances. Typically, interest charges start accruing on the day you withdraw the cash.
Annual fee. In addition to interest, some card issuers charge an annual fee. If you do not want to pay an annual fee, you should ask the issuer for a card that has no fee or try approaching a different card issuer. The credit card market is very competitive and you should be able to shop around for a better deal.
Balance transfers. If you transfer an outstanding balance to your credit card from a different source, interest charges generally start accruing from the day the transfer is effected. There are exceptions, however, so check with your card issuer.
Late payment. Paying beyond the payment due date may also cost you a fee for late payment.
Over the limit. If your total balance goes over your credit limit, you may be charged an extra fee.
Returned cheque. If you pay your credit card bill by cheque and it bounces, you may be charged a fee.
Inactivity. Check to see whether your card issuer charges a fee for not using the card.

Things to Know

- Some card issuers charge a fee for sending reminder letters, duplicate statements, or other correspondence. Be sure to ask about these types of fees when you apply for your card, and keep an eye on future leaflets sent to you because fees can change or new ones can be introduced.

- On the back of each card statement you will find information that tells you about the fees on your card, how to pay, and what to do if you have any queries. Pay particular attention to any additional notes on your statement. They may describe important changes to fees, or may announce special offers, discounts, or payment holidays.

Getting the Best Introductory Rate

Nowadays many card issuers offer low introductory rates in order to get your business. These incentives can be enticing, but check for any drawbacks first.

Check length of terms. The low rate is usually offered only for a short period, typically a few months. Make sure you are aware of any special conditions.

Compare adjustments. Your rate will adjust upwards after the introductory period. Check to see if it will end up being higher than a rate you might get on a card without a low introductory rate.

Read carefully. The terms and conditions will mention whether a late payment will trigger a rise in the interest rate. Check these to protect yourself from high interest rates.

UNDERSTANDING CREDIT CARDS

UNDERSTANDING CREDIT CARD STATEMENTS

Your statement is the best way to track spending, monitor charges, and catch potential errors. It is a snapshot of your account. Formats vary, but generally each statement includes the information shown on the following four pages.

> **27** The date the statement was printed is called the *statement date*.

Account number
This number helps the card issuer identify you. It is usually the same as your card number.

Name
This gives the name and title of the cardholder.

YOUR BANK

Your Bank
Card Services
PO Box 001
Anytown QX00 1YZ

STAT

Name
MS SUSAN THOR

Account number
1234 5555 6789 101

Transaction date
This is a record of the date a transaction took place. It usually takes 3–7 days for a transaction to reach your account. Overseas transactions can take even longer.

transaction date	reference	
		BALANCE BROU(
10 FEB	09876543	PAYMENT REC'D T
25 MAR	01234567	DORLING KINDERS.
26 MAR	02345678	THE GIFT EMPORIUM
28 MAR	03456789	SHOES R US
30 MAR	04567890	THE GREEN PETROL S'
31 MAR	05678901	HATS & COATS BOUTIC

Reference number
This number enables the vendor to identify key details about the transaction, such as which cashier served you.

38

Understanding Credit Card Statements

WHAT YOU OWED AT THE START
Your statement tells you what you owed on the day the billing cycle began.

—

WHAT CREDIT YOU USED
All of your payments, purchases, cash advances, balance transfers, and other transactions are listed in the order they occurred.

=

WHAT YOU OWE NOW
The sum of what you owed at the start, plus the credit you used, determines what you owe now.

▼ SUMMARIZING YOUR ACCOUNT

The items listed on this statement summarize the most important details about your account and the history of recent transactions.

Page number
This tells you the page number of the statement, and how many pages there are in total.

NT OF ACCOUNT

PAGE 1 OF 1

Statement date
6 APRIL

Statement Date
(also called billing date). This is the last day of the statement period and the day the statement was printed. Transactions, charges, and payments after this date will appear on your next statement.

description	amount
ORWARD	1000.00
YOU	1000.00
OOKSHOP) LONDON GBR	8.99
BRIGHTON GBR	12.99
DOVER GBR	45.50
BRIGHTON GBR	25.50
LONDON GBR	75.94

Brought Forward/ Payments Received
These figures summarize how much you owed from the previous statement period, and how much you repaid.

Transaction Amount
This records the exact amount of each transaction, including any repayments you have made to the card issuer. The rest of each line enables you to see the date you made the transaction, the vendor's identifiers, and where the transaction took place.

Description
This section shows the name of the vendor and identifies the place, including the country, where the transaction occurred.

Understanding Credit Cards

What You Need to Pay

Although different card issuers produce differently styled statements, virtually all provide you with the same pieces of information. Most issuers also now give you an estimate of what the next month's interest is likely to be. Here are some guidelines to help you understand this important data.

> **28** Understanding how finance charges are calculated can save you money.

Available Credit
This figure tells you how much you had left to borrow on the day the statement was printed.

Total Credit Limit
The figure given here is the most you can borrow through purchases and cash advances. If you try to go over the limit, the card issuer will probably tell the shop to reject the card. If you have a good payment record, you can ask the issuer to raise your credit limit.

25 MAR	01234567	DORLING KIND
26 MAR	02345678	THE GIFT EMPOR
28 MAR	03456789	SHOES R US
30 MAR	04567890	THE GREEN PETRO
31 MAR	05678901	HATS & COATS BOU

your credit limit	available credit	next month's estimated interest* (see overleaf)
£4000	£3831	£6.38

TAKE PART IN OUR EXCITING CARDHOLDER PRIZE DRAW F
TWO IN VENICE. FIVE RUNNER-UP PRIZES OF A BOTTLE OF
ONE OF THESE PRIZES JUST USE YOUR CREDIT CARD AT LE
MONTH. OTHER METHODS OF ENTRY ALSO AVAILABLE.

Announcements
Many card issuers print announcements on your statements to tell you about forthcoming special offers, discounts, promotions, prizes, and payment holidays. Keep an eye out for them.

Next month's estimated interest
Many card issuers now give an estimate of what next month's interest is likely to be. This figure is based on the following assumptions: the sum you owe does not increase, you pay the minimum payment on the due date, and the interest rate remains the same. If there are any changes to these, the interest amount will vary accordingly.

UNDERSTANDING CREDIT CARD STATEMENTS

> **29** If you suspect that any charges are not correct, contact the card issuer immediately.

CALCULATING INTEREST CHARGES

Credit card issuers usually calculate interest charges in one of the following four ways:

Average daily balance. This method takes your balances each day during the billing period, adds them all together, and divides by the number of days in the billing period. The periodic interest rate is then used to calculate the finance charge for that period.

Adjusted balance. With this method, the card issuer subtracts payments you make during the billing period from your balance at the beginning of that period. This means your balance is kept lower and you pay less in finance charges.

Previous balance. The card issuer applies the monthly finance charge to your starting balance for the billing period. Any purchases and payments during the month are not included.

Ending balance. The card issuer uses your ending balance for the period. Any purchases and payments during the billing period are included.

(BOOKSHOP)	LONDON	GBR	8.99
	BRIGHTON	GBR	12.99
	DOVER	GBR	45.50
ION	BRIGHTON	GBR	25.50
	LONDON	GBR	75.94

ninimum yment of	to reach us by	your balance
8.45	3 MAY	£168.92

HANCE TO WIN A WEEKEND FOR
AGNE. FOR A CHANCE TO WIN
REE TIMES DURING THE NEXT
AVAILABLE ON REQUEST.

Minimum Payment
This figure is the minimum you must pay before the due date. If you pay less than this amount by the date specified, a negative mark will be added to your credit report. In addition to extra interest, you may also have to pay a fee for late payment.

Your Balance
This is the amount you owed on the day the statement was printed. It includes any sums repaid and cleared before the statement date.

Payment Due Date
The card issuer must receive at least the minimum payment by this date. If paying by post, you should allow at least 7 working days for the payment to reach your account. If paying at a bank, allow 5 working days.

UNDERSTANDING CREDIT CARDS

CALCULATING CHARGES

This is an example of how the interest is calculated on card purchases. Some credit card issuers have a different way of calculating interest. If you do not pay off the debt by the end of the grace period, some issuers charge you interest from the end of the period, while others backdate it to the date of purchase. Some card issuers also charge you interest on the whole debt, even if you have paid off part of it.

▼ USING THE GRACE PERIOD

Some issuers give you 20–25 days at the end of the billing cycle to pay the balance on your card. If you start the period with a balance of £0 and settle any transactions in full by the due date, you will pay no interest.

£4.56 interest

Day 3. A £20 purchase.
Day 15. No new purchases.
Day 25. A £2,000 purchase.
Day 28. No new purchases.

1. Calculate amount owed each day.
2. Total all those amounts for the period.
3. Divide the total by the number of days in the period.

Average daily balance = £304.28.

Grace period. You make no payments.

Late payment. If you pass the grace period, you will pay interest at the daily periodic rate (in this example the rate of interest is 18% a year, or 1.5% a month). Interest = £304.28 x 1.5% = £4.56

day 28 — No new purchases

Grace Period

Late Payment Period

day 3 — £20 purchase
day 1 — £0
day 15 — No new purchases
day 25 — £2,000 purchase

Billing Cycle

CALCULATING CHARGES

▼ WORKING OUT INTEREST CHARGES

Although there are different ways to calculate interest charges, many major card issuers favour a method called average daily balance. *The method is as follows:*
1) Calculate the amount owed each day.
2) Total all those amounts for the period;
3) Divide the total by the number of days in the period.

Most major card issuers also use a method called daily periodic rate *to charge interest. Interest is added to your account daily, increasing your average daily balance even if you do not make any new purchases. Essentially, you are charged interest on the interest you owe and have not yet paid.*

UNDERSTANDING BILLING PERIODS

A billing period (or billing cycle) is the period of time covered on one statement, usually between 28 and 31 days. Billing cycles often vary between card issuers, so check to see when your card's billing period begins and ends.

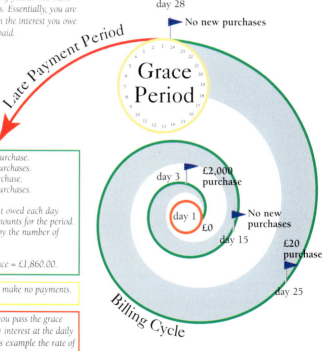

£27.90 interest

Day 3. A £2,000 purchase.
Day 15. No new purchases.
Day 25. A £20 purchase.
Day 28. No new purchases.

1. Calculate amount owed each day.
2. Total all those amounts for the period.
3. Divide the total by the number of days in the period.

Average daily balance = £1,860.00.

Grace period. *You make no payments.*

Late payment. *If you pass the grace period, you will pay interest at the daily periodic rate (in this example the rate of interest is 18% a year, or 1.5% a month). Interest = £1,860.00 x 1.5% = £27.90*

UNDERSTANDING CREDIT CARDS

EXPLORING CARD BENEFITS

Credit cards come with other benefits besides readily available credit. Depending on the card issuer and the level of credit you receive, you may get a wide range of additional benefits, all free of charge.

GETTING THE BEST FROM YOUR CARD

The sales brochure and the introductory package will tell you which of these benefits are included with your card:
- Guaranteed hotel reservations.
- Double the manufacturer's warranty and an extended service agreement on many products.
- Free collision cover on car rentals.
- Travel and emergency assistance, including medical and legal referrals when travelling, arranging emergency transport to hospitals, or travel for your children.
- Assistance with replacing lost tickets or luggage.
- Interpreters to help you in person or on the phone.
- Delivery assistance for prescriptions, valuable documents, emergency cash, and card replacements.
- Other travel assistance, from lists of ATM locations and weather reports to legal and health requirements in your destination.
- Insurance against damage or loss for items worth over a specified amount when purchased with your card. Ask your card issuer for details.

30 A good credit history will open the way to more benefits and rewards.

EXPLORING CARD BENEFITS

USING GOLD AND PLATINUM CARDS

Many card issuers offer premier versions of their credit cards to people with high incomes and/or excellent credit records. Gold and platinum cards typically offer:
- Higher credit lines, so you can buy more before hitting your limit.
- Benefits that are not available to standard cardholders.
- A lower interest rate, although you might have to pay an annual fee or forfeit the grace period.

THINGS TO KNOW

- Many cards come with offers of added protection, which are essentially insurance in case you cannot meet your credit card repayments due to hardship. Cover could include involuntary unemployment, disability, or hospitalization. Be sure to evaluate the fees and terms and conditions carefully to determine if this protection is worth it.

- You may be used to throwing away enclosures such as The Disclosure of Changes to the Terms and Conditions of Your Card, but it pays to review them. Card issuers always have to disclose any changes they make to a card's benefits or its fees. If you know what your card offers, you will avoid surprises at inopportune moments and take advantage of new opportunities.

KEEPING YOUR CREDIT SAFE

Having two different credit cards and keeping one at home and one in your bag or wallet means that you will always have credit available, even if your home is robbed or your bag or wallet is stolen. If your cash is stolen, keeping one of your credit cards in a separate place is a wise precaution in case of emergencies.

31 Some cards may cost more if they offer extra benefits or rewards.

UNDERSTANDING CREDIT CARDS

USING OTHER CARDS

Some cards offer special advantages. There is a card to meet just about any special interest or use.

PAYING BY SMART CARD

These cards are clever credit cards. Although smart cards are not yet widely available in Britain, they are becoming popular in Europe. One system called *Mondex* is particularly clever. The card has a microchip, instead of the usual magnetic strip, which contains a virtual wallet into which money is credited. Retailers can use a special machine to take money out of the customer's virtual wallet and pay it into their own. Smart cards can carry a wide range of personal data, and you can choose the information you wish to load, as follows:

- Electronic cash as an alternative to cash. It is a secure and convenient way to pay. Simply swipe your card through a special machine, and the cash is deducted from your card (not from an account).
- Travel preferences, such as seating and meals. If you use the card to buy a ticket, your preferences are included automatically.
- Discount programmes from retailers and merchants you use regularly. Any discounts awarded will be calculated automatically when you pay with your smart card.

ACCESSING BENEFITS

People in Belgium use smart cards to access health insurance benefits, which reportedly reduces the cost of processing claims by between 65 and 80 per cent.

32 Many speciality cards charge special fees. Always check that the fees are worth any advantages they offer.

Using Other Cards

Using Reward Cards

Many reward cards have the name of a partner, such as a major brand retailer or service provider, displayed on them. These are *co-branded cards*, which give you a way to use credit and earn points towards a reward, a rebate, or some other benefit. Every time you use a card sponsored by an airline, for example, you may earn points towards free flights. A card sponsored by a supermarket may earn you money off your next shopping bill.

> **33** Shopping around will help you find a speciality card that is just right for you.

Opting for Cashback Cards

These cards give you back a small percentage of your purchases as cash. Since retailers have to pay the card issuer a percentage of the value of the transaction, these cards effectively share the card issuer's commission with the cardholder. Sometimes card issuers change the amount they will pay you, so check your card statements and enclosures regularly for any changes.

Deciding to Use Affinity Cards

Card issuers offer cards that carry the logo of all kinds of organizations. These are called *affinity cards*. Consumers usually choose these cards because of an emotional, intellectual, or psychological attachment to the group or lifestyle represented on the card. If you like a particular flying club, for example, you might want to use that club's branded card. An affinity card sponsored by an association might mean that every pound you spend generates a small donation to a worthy cause, perhaps to a charity or your favourite football team. There are many affinity cards available. Check the terms to see whether you will be paying higher fees or rates than on your current card and whether the trade-off is worth it to you.

Helping Charities

Affinity cards can be valuable money-raisers for charities. For example, they have raised over £5 million for the RSPB (Royal Society for Protection of Birds) and over £1.5 million for Oxfam.

Knowing Your Rights

Your rights are usually listed in the card's conditions of use. Important among them are your rights to correct problems.

34 The phone number for reporting a lost or stolen card is on the back of every statement.

35 The Consumer Credit Act protects you from errors and fraud by merchants when using your card.

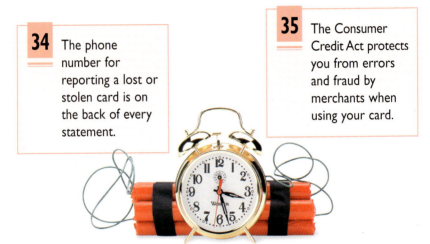

Dealing with Unauthorized Use

Report theft immediately. If you report the theft immediately, you will not usually be held liable for any transactions made without your consent. If you fail to report the card missing within a stipulated time, however, or act negligently in a way that causes loss that was avoidable, you may be liable for part or all of any transactions made.

Card protection. For a small fee, many card issuers offer a protection service for lost or stolen cards. When considering whether this is worth the fee, keep in mind the cost of the service compared with your potential liability.

Disputes on your card. If you have a dispute about a charge on your credit card bill, you should raise the matter immediately with the credit card issuer. If you ordered goods but never received them, or the goods were faulty, they may allow you to defer payment while the matter is sorted out, or temporarily refund the amount to your account until the merchant supplies proof of entitlement to it. However, they can also insist on payment by the due date. It is best to talk to the card issuer as early as possible and try to come to an amicable arrangement.

KNOWING YOUR RIGHTS

BUYING FROM HOME

With increasing amounts of people shopping on the internet and by telephone, it is important to understand your rights when buying from home. Under the Distance Selling Regulations, home shoppers have some special rights. These include:
- Clear information before placing an order.
- A cooling-off period in most cases.
- A full refund if goods or services are not provided by an agreed date or within 30 days of placing an order if no date was agreed.

However, there are exemptions for some services. To check your rights, contact the Office of Fair Trading or consult their website at www.oft.gov.uk.

36 Never keep your PIN number with your card – you might be held liable for any losses.

GETTING PROTECTION

By law, every product must work properly if used for its intended purpose. When you use a credit card to buy a product, you usually get a form of buyer protection that helps you dispute charges that are:
- Above the agreed price.
- For items ordered but never received.
- For wrong items.
- For items that do not work as intended.
- For unsatisfactory services.

For that reason it is often a good idea to buy things with your credit card, even if you have cash or a cheque available. This is especially true when buying expensive items such as holidays or furniture. Do not rely on credit cards to solve all your consumer problems, however. Even if the credit card issuer does help you to get compensation or your money back, it can take a long time and involve a lot of hassle. Nonetheless, credit cards can provide you with valuable protection if something goes wrong. So where possible, use your credit card to pay for expensive items. It will increase your consumer protection.

Protecting Your Credit

There are many methods you can use to protect your credit. The most important thing is to be aware of your credit history and know how to avoid problems that may arise.

Monitoring Your Credit File

Here are some of the methods you can use to correct errors in your file.

1. Obtain a Copy of Your File

You are entitled to see your credit file at any time. It will usually cost very little. In recent years, files have cost as little as £2.00 each.

2. Write or Telephone

You can make a request in writing, by telephone, or even over the internet. If you just want a copy of your file, you may find it more convenient to telephone. However, if you have a dispute, writing may be a better option. You can write down your issues and review them, to make sure you are stating your case clearly.

3. Use Recorded Delivery

If you prefer, you can send the request letter by recorded delivery, which will give you proof of delivery. Your local post office will tell you how to do this, if you do not already know. Copy the letter and the cheque for the file. Date and file them, so you can refer to them later.

Monitoring Your Credit File

4. Wait 7 Days

Credit reference agencies are legally obliged to send a copy of your credit file to you within 7 working days of receiving your request. If you have not received a copy of your file by then, telephone the helpdesk, where they should be able to trace the progress of your request.

5. Check Your File Carefully

When you receive your file, check it carefully. If you think that anything is wrong, write to the credit reference agency asking for the entry to be removed or deleted, stating your reasons why. Under the **Consumer Credit Act 1974**, the agency must write within 28 days and tell you that the entry has been removed or deleted, or that no action has been taken.

6. Request a Revised Copy

If your credit file has been amended, you are entitled to a corrected copy at no extra charge. If you still disagree with the contents, you are entitled to include a 200-word "Notice of Correction" of your own in your credit file, as long as you send it within 28 days. Lenders are obliged to take a notice of correction into account. It takes your application out of the automatic credit scoring procedure, to be assessed individually. However, it should be worded carefully.

7. Take Further Action

If the agency does not accept your Notice of Correction, it will normally refer it on to the Information Commissioner on your behalf. If not, you can write to: Information Commissioner, Wycliffe House, Water Lane, Wilmslow, Cheshire SK9 5AF.

---

37 Credit reference agencies and lenders are regulated by the Office of Fair Trading.

Asking for a Notice of Disassociation

If you can prove you are not financially connected with someone who has got into financial difficulties, you can ask the agency to put a Notice of Disassociation on your file. Give full names and addresses of those involved, and the nature of your relationship.

38 You may dispute your credit file if you believe that any of the contents are inaccurate or obsolete.

39 If you are still unhappy with your credit file, contact your local Citizens Advice Bureau.

Keeping Watch over Your Credit

Your credit file is a reflection of your finances, so it is worth looking after it. Credit experts offer the following tips for removing errors.

Monitoring the File

The time to check your credit file and sort out any inconsistencies or errors is before you apply for a loan. It is a lot better than waiting for surprises and discovering at the last minute that you have been denied the loan.

Correcting Errors

Trying to correct problems on your credit file yourself can be risky. You can make matters worse if you are not well organized and precise in your dealings with the credit reference agencies. If you do not feel comfortable doing it yourself, you should contact a credit counselling group for help. Some experts believe that the risks of doing it yourself include:

- Confirming negative statements, or even adding new, unfavourable information unintentionally.
- Making statements that trigger an alert for fraud or other concerns.
- Wasting time on strategies that experts know will not work.
- Using forms from self-help books that can lead to misleading statements, or that will not be taken as seriously as a personal, typewritten letter.

LABELLING DISPUTES

Always indicate clearly in writing whether you are challenging an entry because it is "not mine" or "not late".

CHECKING FOR MISTAKES

Experts advise you to look for common errors when checking your credit file such as:
- Items that belong to someone with the same surname.
- Duplicate information.
- Incorrect items that have not been removed or items that have stayed on your file too long.

 Keep copies of all letters between you and the credit reference agency.

EXERCISING CAUTION

Any authorized organizations with legitimate needs may request a copy of your credit file. This includes car dealers, insurance companies, banks, mortgage companies, and other legitimate organizations, even if you did not give a written release authorizing the enquiry. Employers and landlords can look only at public information on your file, and you get a copy before they see it.

THINGS TO DO

- Make a list of all your valuable cards and any important documents and keep it in a safe place, such as a safety deposit box. For each card include the issuer's name and telephone number, and your account number. In an emergency you may need to refer to this list quickly. Having to reconstruct this list after your cards have been lost could be frustrating and time consuming and may cause you further delays in securing your credit from theft.

- When dealing with a dispute, keep a file containing copies of all letters, mark your calendar for important dates, and take down names and titles of every person with whom you speak. Keep a record of what is said. Send letters by recorded delivery so that you have proof of when and where they were received.

- If you suspect that someone has assumed or attempted to assume your identity, contact the credit reference agencies and any other organizations that may have been used by the impersonator. The agencies will be able to help you identify how far the fraud has gone. They can also add security features to your file, such as adding a password that only you and the agency know. Whenever a credit check is conducted, you will then be asked to provide the correct password. Even if the impersonator has stolen your driving licence or credit cards, he or she will not be able to use your identity without knowing the password.

◀ ESCALATING FRAUD
With the advent of the internet, unauthorized requests for credit files have increased.

Identifying Unfair Credit Practices

Some credit practices are unfair to consumers. In some cases they can even be misleading or illegal.

Insisting on a Minimum Purchase

This is not unfair, misleading, or illegal, but it is valuable to know. Some shops require a minimum purchase amount before they accept your card: this is due to the charge they will incur from the card issuer. Usually they do not charge more than the retail price.

> **41** You should check a credit deal as carefully as you check your main purchase.

Using Personal Data without Permission

You should always be very careful about giving out your personal information. Not only can it be used by organizations who wish to target you for commercial reasons, it can also be used by unscrupulous people to gain access to your bank accounts and credit cards. To make life as difficult as possible for thieves, keep PINs and passwords separate from your cards and cheque books.

Charging a High Rate of Interest

Some lenders charge extortionate rates of interest. If you have borrowed money at a much higher interest rate than that normally available, you may be able to change the agreement by applying to the county court in England and Wales, or the sheriff's court in Scotland. However, the chances of success are low unless the case is exceptional, and not all loans fall under the jurisdiction of the courts. If you are unsure, you should seek legal advice from your local Citizens Advice Bureau first to see whether or not the courts can be of help. You can find the address of your nearest Citizens Advice Bureau in your local telephone book.

IDENTIFYING UNFAIR CREDIT PRACTICES

MAKING BOGUS TELEPHONE CALLS

Often thieves make bogus telephone calls in order to commit fraud. Do not give your credit card details to anyone who has telephoned you. Ask for the caller's telephone number and other identifying information, then check it. Legitimate organizations will be able to give you checkable credentials.

RUNNING MARKETING SCAMS AND CONTESTS

There are many scams (and legal but misleading marketing campaigns) that guarantee you have won a prize with no obligation to buy, or offer tremendous discounts if you telephone right away. This is a big problem area for law enforcement and consumers because the offers seem so tempting that people want to believe they are winning something for free, despite their better judgment.

▲ STOPPING THIEVES
If your credit card goes missing, you should report it to the card issuer immediately. Some companies also offer a service that registers the details of all your cards so that, if your purse or wallet is stolen, you simply need to make one telephone call to them and they will call everyone on your behalf.

42 Fraud accounted for over £370 million in illegal transactions in Europe last year.

KNOWING WHERE TO COMPLAIN

If you think a shop or other organization has acted unfairly, you can report it to your local trading standards office. Credit card associations also want to know about violations of their rules. Start with a call to the organization that issued your card. If you are not satisfied, try the relevant credit card association, such as MasterCard or Visa.

Managing Your Debt

How much debt can you handle? The answer is different for everyone. How you handle debt can affect you for a long time, so you should be aware of the advantages and pitfalls of debt.

Borrowing Wisely

Many experts recommend that no more than 15–20% of your monthly household income should be committed to credit card minimum payments and other loan payments, excluding rent or a mortgage. Furthermore, no more than 40% of your monthly income should go to paying all debts, including rent or a mortgage.

Keeping Loans Manageable

In most cases, lenders have a level of comfort with your credit. They will lend you only as much as they feel they can risk and you can afford. Typically you can borrow three times your annual salary for a home. However, much depends on other factors such as your credit history.

◀ STAYING OUT OF THE RED
A sure way to manage debt is to try to stay out of debt entirely – something not too many people can do these days.

Borrowing Wisely

43 If you extend yourself too far into debt, you will be *overextended* and in danger of being unable to repay on schedule.

Things to Know

- Some experts work out how much you should use your credit to take on debt by calculating what is called a *credit ratio analysis*. This is also a measure of your financial abilities. The ratio is calculated by assessing what percentage of your monthly income is taken up with your expenses.

- A low ratio is under 20%, which means that the person is in good financial health and is doing a good job of managing finances.

- A moderate ratio is between 21% and 40%. This may mean that the person should look carefully at his or her monthly expenses and start decreasing the overall level of debt, including credit cards.

- A high ratio is over 40%. This may mean that the person should immediately stop accumulating debt and start looking for ways to decrease the total debt to a more manageable level.

Deciding How Much You Can Borrow

In order to determine what amount of credit is right for you, follow this calculation:

Income. Add up all your income for one year, whether it comes from a job (after taxes), state benefits, scholarships, support from parents or spouse, or any other source. Divide this number by 12 to get your monthly income.

Expenses. Add up all your expenses including rent, loan repayments, car payments, insurance premiums, clothing, travelling costs, and utilities, then calculate their monthly cost.

Surplus. Subtract what you spend (expenses) from what you receive (income) in order to determine exactly how much you have left over each month.

For example, if you make £2,000 per month and you spend £1,500, you will have £500 left over. You may choose to save this money, or you may decide to leverage your buying power by taking out a loan that costs you less than the £500 surplus you have each month.

Getting Help with Debt

If you cannot resolve a debt directly with a creditor, or you are not sure what to do, you should consider enlisting help from a reputable, non-profitmaking credit counselling service.

Finding Experts You Can Trust

Here are some trustworthy services associated with non-profit organizations:

- Your local Citizens Advice Bureau gives free advice and help – look in your local telephone book.
- The Consumer Credit Counselling Service (CCCS) is supported partly by the credit industry. It will provide a counsellor to act as a go-between with your creditors and arrange a workable repayment plan. Telephone 0800 138 1111 or look up the website at www.cccs.co.uk.
- Call National Debt Helpline on 0808 808 4000, or send an e-mail to advice@nationaldebtline.co.uk.
- Try the Federation of Independent Advice Centres at 4 Deans Court, St. Paul's Churchyard, London EC4V 5AA. Telephone 020 7489 1800. Website: www.fiac.org.uk.
- Contact Credit Action at 6 Regent Terrace, Cambridge CB2 1AA. Helpline: 0800 591084. Website: www.creditaction.com.

44 Get help quickly. Waiting will usually make your situation worse.

Getting Help with Debt

Exploring the Alternatives

You have other options apart from contacting consumer counselling services. They are:

Mediation. Using a neutral third party to help you and the creditor open a line of communication and resolve your dispute can be very helpful. It is very informal. The mediator cannot force either side in the dispute to do anything.

Arbitration. You and the creditor may agree to argue a disputed charge before a neutral third party (often a lawyer or judge). If the disputed sum is not large, the process is informal and may not require a lawyer. Both of you are bound by the decision, and the winner may get a refund of the arbitration fee.

Litigation. This is the most expensive and most aggressive choice. A lawyer can negotiate or fight a legal battle for you, if necessary. For example, you can tell a collection agency to speak only with your lawyer if you want to avoid calls at home.

Arranging a Debt Management Plan

Using a Debt Management Plan, a counsellor can create a workable budget with you and negotiate with creditors to reduce your monthly payments and extend the time to catch up on any missed payments. The counsellor may also be able to negotiate waived or lowered interest rates while you are on the plan. Each month you send your counsellor the amount necessary to pay your creditors. It is held in a special account and cheques are posted to your creditors weekly or monthly. You will be required to stop further borrowing until your debts are under control.

Things to Know

- Some advice centres will charge for helping you, so make sure you know exactly what you are getting into before you accept their services. Some organizations may negotiate much smaller debt repayments. This might be of help, but you may end up paying more over a longer period of time, and your credit record may be affected. So make sure you know what the long-term implications of any rescheduled payments might be.

- Be wary of advertisements from organizations claiming to be able to remove negative information from your credit file for a fee. Virtually all of them can do only what you can do yourself, and they may make the situation worse. You do not have to pay for guidance on doing it yourself – you can get it for free.

- Some credit repair services or credit consultants may charge high fees for work that should not be done at all. For example, they may dispute accurate items on your credit report just to see if they can find a way to have items removed. This could lead to more trouble instead of less, as well as costing you unnecessary fees. If the negative information is legitimate, the only way to handle it is to deal with your debt.

45 The best way to clear debt is to earn more and reduce expenses.

Understanding Debt Collection Practices

If all else fails, a lender will turn over your account to its collection department or a collection agency.

Collecting your Debt

The last resort of any creditor, other than suing you (which may not be economically feasible), is to hand over your debt to a collection agency. These agencies are not interested in keeping you as a customer. The collector may start by sending you a notice. If you do not respond, telephone calls will begin. If you try to work out a repayment plan with the collector and get nowhere, contact the creditor again and explain your plan. Collectors may try to use aggressive tactics. By law, however, there are limits to what they can do or say to collect from you.

46 Lenders pay collection agencies to recoup as much debt as they can – not to help you.

Understanding Debt Collection Practices

Handling Debt Collectors

When dealing with debt collectors, here are some tips:

Never get angry. Losing your temper with a debt collector may only make your situation worse.

Never send a postdated cheque. It makes your payment offer conditional and does not help resolve the problem.

Document all conversations. Include the name of the collector, the date and time of the telephone call, and exactly what was discussed and agreed.

Get everything in writing. Ask the debt collector to post or fax the agreed settlement to you immediately.

Try negotiating. Try to settle the debts for half to two-thirds of the amount you owe. The collector will still make money and you will save money.

Hang up if necessary. If a collector becomes abusive on the telephone, do not stay on the line.

File a complaint. If you feel your rights have been violated, first write to the company concerned. If it is not resolved, seek free advice from the Citizens Advice Bureau.

Knowing about Bailiffs' Rights

The law surrounding bailiffs is complex and is currently subject to Government review. However, here is a guide provided by the Citizens Advice Bureau:

- In most cases, bailiffs cannot take essential goods, for example beds and cooking equipment.
- It is good practice for bailiffs to refer cases back to the court or creditor where it is obvious that there is nothing of value on the premises or where the debtor is particularly vulnerable.
- In general, bailiffs should charge only fees that are reasonable bearing in mind the activities undertaken – their fees can be challenged in the courts.
- In consumer debt cases it is possible to apply to the court to suspend the actions of the bailiff and pay by instalments.
- Letters that resemble a court summons or other official document are sometimes issued by creditors or debt collection agencies. Using documents like this could be a criminal offence under the County Courts Act 1984 and the Administration of Justice Act 1970.

Managing Your Debt

Consolidating Debts

You may want to consolidate your debts into a single loan. If you are having difficulty paying your debts, there may be some advantages to getting a consolidation loan. It all depends upon your specific situation.

Understanding Consolidation

A consolidation loan merges your existing loans into a single loan. This type of loan creates one regular payment, usually monthly, for all your debts.

One advantage is that if you can successfully consolidate your loans, you may be able to avoid bankruptcy.

Why would a creditor want to agree to this? Remember, it is to a creditor's advantage to help you pay back your loan. The creditor would rather have a reduced rate, especially where there is still profit to be made from your loan, than receive nothing at all and have to sue you to get the money back.

This can work to your advantage. Your payments are reduced, and you only have to make one convenient monthly payment to the consolidation company for all the loans that have been consolidated. If you are considering a consolidation loan, always negotiate and shop around in order to get the lowest interest rate and monthly repayments possible. Make sure you read the fine print, and check the credentials of the loan consolidation company very carefully before going ahead.

47 Be careful who you select: some consolidators are not reputable.

Making Loan Offers

Lenders send loan consolidation offers to anyone whose name and address they can get. It does not mean the lender knows anything about you or your credit history yet. In most cases, you still have to fill out an application and be evaluated as you would for any other loan.

48 Spending the money saved by consolidating debts will only increase your monthly payments again.

CONSOLIDATING DEBTS

EVALUATING AN OFFER

Below is a typical example of a loan consolidation direct mail offer. To begin analyzing an offer, check whether it provides information on the four basic parts of a loan, as follows:

1. How much can you borrow? In the case below, the lender is willing to let you borrow £60,000.
2. What will it cost? The annual percentage rate (APR) in this case is 13.38%.
3. What is the repayment plan? Your repayments will be due once a month.
4. What if you do not repay? This offer does not give this information.

There is a lot of other information missing from this offer. Read the fine print, and check out the lender and the offer carefully to be sure you understand everything before you commit yourself.

USING THE EQUITY IN YOUR HOME

Many loan offers for debt consolidation are actually home equity loans. Lenders feel safer offering you a loan with a relatively low interest rate (or a higher interest rate if your credit record has trouble spots) because you are required to put up your home as security. You should always seek independent financial advice before putting up your home as security for a loan. If in doubt, consult your local Citizens Advice Bureau.

Dear Homeowner

You may be eligible for a special home loan that will consolidate your debts into *one low monthly payment*. This unique programme will allow you to receive these funds *even if your property has no equity!*

Money Ltd. is introducing this **Debt Consolidation Loan** exclusively to preselected homeowners in your area. Best of all, *you can use these funds for any purpose*, such as home improvements, paying off your car loan or credit cards, having a holiday, or just extra cash!

Obtaining your loan is quick and easy, and savings can begin with a single telephone call. *There are absolutely NO up-front costs and NO risks to you.* Your funds can be available in as little as 7–10 working days.

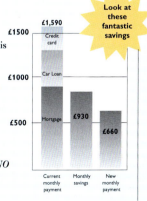

Handling Excessive Debt

If you feel you are being overwhelmed by debt, you need to find a way to get out of it. Making an effort to pay your bills will help lenders see that you are aware of the problem and that your promise is still worth something.

Controlling Debt

Here are a few suggestions from experts on avoiding, controlling, and reducing debt:

Refinance high-cost loans. Refinancing loans that charge high interest rates can immediately reduce your payments and save you money.

Make a budget. Start by writing down all the ways you spend money, including small cash expenses. If you cannot pay your debts, see which expenses you can reduce or even eliminate altogether.

Pay off high-interest debt first. If you cannot refinance your debts, pay off the loans with the highest interest rate first. These will cost you the most in the long run.

Use credit cards cautiously. They can be a convenient substitute for cash, but you need to be disciplined and pay them off every month to avoid more debt. If you cannot pay them off immediately, pledge to pay them off completely within a specified time and recheck your spending habits.

Build an emergency fund. Having three to six month's expenses in the bank can prevent disaster. If something happens to you, such as unemployment, disability, or hospitalization and you have no income, this will help pay your expenses while you get back on your feet.

Find ways to save. Once you are free of debt, look into ways you can save your money instead of how you can spend it.

Getting Help

Sometimes you cannot get out of debt. Situations beyond your control can arise and overwhelm you. Relationship breakdown, unemployment, or a loss of business can happen to anyone. Many lenders will offer help and protection if they see you are genuinely trying to remedy the situation.

49 Saving your money will increase your buying power in the long run.

HANDLING EXCESSIVE DEBT

CONTACTING LENDERS

Maintaining a good relationship with lenders will help you stay in control of your credit.

Keep in touch. If you stay on good terms with your creditors while you have financial problems, they are far more willing to help you rebuild your credit. The creditor who reported the default is the only one who can remove the negative mark from your credit report. Get any agreements with creditors in writing. Send a copy of the agreement to the credit reference agency.

Deal with the lender directly. If you have tried to correct a dispute in your credit report and the credit reference agency is not cooperating, contact the creditor directly. If you are successful, a letter to the agency accompanied by the creditor's agreement in writing, should resolve the problem.

FACING YOUR CREDITORS ▼
Do not bury your head: face your creditors and work out a plan. This can keep them from reporting the situation to a credit reference agency and preserve your creditworthiness.

DEALING WITH PROBLEMS

Try to deal with problems promptly or they will rapidly get worse.

Face up to the situation. If you are late paying, creditors typically send standard letters to you as polite reminders. If you still do not pay, they may send more letters with increasing intensity or they may telephone you. Eventually they will make demands, backed by the threat of legal action or the use of a debt collection agency.

Work it out. Your creditors are motivated by two needs: to be repaid and to keep you as a customer. These tend to work in your favour. If you default on a debt, the creditor might in some cases require you to repay the entire debt at once. That rarely happens, however, because the lender is interested in building a relationship with you and making more loans, not in ruining your credit record.

Ask the creditor for help. Most creditors are willing to listen if you ask for help in structuring a new repayment plan. For example, they may grant you an extension of time or reduce repayment amounts (but increase the number of payments).

Set up a payment plan. Contact the creditor as soon as you know you will not be able to make a payment. Utility companies, such as electricity and gas suppliers, are used to dealing with people who have difficulty paying, and may be able to help.

MANAGING YOUR DEBT

UNDERSTANDING BANKRUPTCY

Bankruptcy should be used only as a last resort. Make sure you understand what it involves and the implications of being bankrupt.

DEFINING BANKRUPTCY

Bankruptcy is a legal declaration of your inability to repay your debts. When you file for bankruptcy, you are telling your creditors you cannot pay them back at this time, but you are putting together a plan to pay them back partially or fully. Most creditors will be more interested in finding a way to get back their money than in forcing you into bankruptcy. Although you may prefer to avoid the intrusion, stigma, and future credit problems bankruptcy brings, this is sometimes the best solution. Once you apply to the court, all collection efforts against you must stop. You are not allowed to take on any new debts, and the court will freeze your assets.

50 Bankruptcy protects you from creditors while you reorganize your debts.

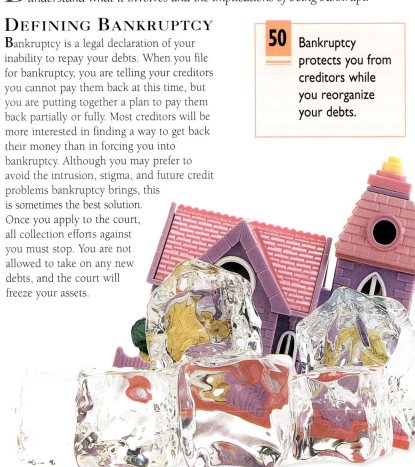

Declaring Bankruptcy

You can be made bankrupt either by the people to whom you owe money or by declaring yourself bankrupt. Bankruptcy petitions are made either in the local county court or, if the business has traded in London, in the high court. Being declared bankrupt can have serious effects on your future. A bankrupt cannot practise law, become a Justice of the Peace, a Member of Parliament, or a trustee of a charity.

Appointing a Receiver

An official receiver is appointed to administer your assets and protect them. The receiver may work with an insolvency practitioner to dispose of your assets and attempt to pay off some of the debts. You will therefore have to supply complete details of your assets so that the receiver can assess which debts can be paid off and how best to handle the sale of any goods you possess. You will also be required to supply details of all your creditors, and attend interviews with the receiver in which your financial situation will be discussed and analyzed. The receiver will take over payments to your creditors so that in general you will not have control over which bills should be paid.

Ending Bankruptcy

If your unsecured debts are less than £20,000, you will be discharged from bankruptcy after two years. The term extends to three years if your debts are over £20,000. However, there are exceptions and in some cases the term will be five years, so check with the official receiver's office.

Abiding by the Regulations

Generally, bankrupts are discharged from their bankruptcy after two or three years, although this can be extended. Once you are discharged, you will be released from most of your debts. Laws and rules change and you must take professional advice about the requirements upon you before, during, and after your bankruptcy. It is impossible to give all the rules here, but one of the most important states that you must not apply for credit facilities or borrow money from anyone while you are bankrupt. Acting improperly may mean you are committing a criminal offence. Although bankruptcy can help close the door on a painful financial past, it is a serious matter and you should consider it carefully with professional help before embarking on any bankruptcy proceedings.

Filing for Bankruptcy

Here is information on how to file for bankruptcy and what it means to your credit history. It is important to understand what you may and may not do while you are bankrupt in order to avoid further problems later.

Getting Started

Obtain the forms and fill them out. Try to get good professional guidance if possible. If you really cannot afford a lawyer or other professional, you can try using forms from the local court. The court may be able to suggest low-cost or free assistance to help you with your filing. It is worth asking. You will be required to verify your:
- Income and property owned.
- Debts.
- Monthly living expenses.
- Property you are claiming as exempt.

File the forms with the local court. Although amounts vary, the filing fee will be around £120, and the services of the official receiver will cost approximately £250.

Attend a creditors meeting. After you have filed for bankruptcy and the court has reviewed your case, you will be required to attend a creditors meeting and face the people you owe. The creditors can show up and state their cases before the trustee, who then decides what is to be done. Since there usually is not enough money for everyone, creditors will probably have to accept a fraction of what they are owed. This is the worst result of breaking your promise to repay because it breaks the bond of trust.

Investigating Fraud

Bankruptcy courts know that some people try to use them to avoid debts and keep their money. If you have transferred property, withdrawn lots of cash, or bought luxury items just before filing for bankruptcy, a court will investigate the possibility that you committed fraud. If the creditor finds out, it will probably take action. It is also an offence not to disclose assets, or to fail to account for their loss. In severe cases, bankrupts can be sent to prison.

51 Creditors with secured loans are first in line to be repaid from the sale of property.

Deciding What You May Keep

Once you have been declared bankrupt, you will lose control of most of your assets. However, there are some exceptions. Basic items like some clothing, furniture, bedding, and tools of your trade might still be left with you. However, you must still declare all the assets and the receiver will decide what you can keep and what must be surrendered. Depending on the specific circumstances of your bankruptcy, your home may also be sold in order to pay off your debts. Also, any registration or licence that you have obtained in connection with your work might be affected by the bankruptcy order. You should inform the issuing organization of your bankrupt status to see whether the registration or licence can remain in force.

Repairing Your Credit

When you begin applying for credit again, some lenders will consider you too great a risk. Any lenders who do offer you credit will insist on charging you a higher interest rate for the loan than they would offer to more creditworthy borrowers. By making regular and prompt repayments, you can gradually rebuild a positive credit profile. However, you may not be considered a good credit risk until several years have expired.

52 People who are bankrupt do not pay bills directly. Creditors must apply to the receiver for payment.

Exploring Alternatives to Bankruptcy

Instead of becoming bankrupt, you might want to consider an administration order or an individual voluntary agreement (IVA). These arrangements can offer you different options and you should take advice on them before making any decisions.

INDEX

A
account numbers, 38, 53
adjusted balance method, 41
Administration Order, 69
advice, 51, 58–9
affinity cards, 47
agencies, credit reference, 16–21, 51–3
annual fees, 22, 37
applications, 12–13, 17
arbitration, 59
assets, 13, 25, 69
ATM cards, 33
average daily balance, 41–3

B
bailiffs, 61
balance transfers, 37
Bank of England, 8, 9
bankruptcy, 16, 19, 66–9
base rate, 8
benefits, credit cards, 44–5
billing cycle, 42–3
billing date, 39
blacklists, 18
bonds, 9
borrowing, 15, 57
see also loans
bounced cheques, 37
budgeting, 6, 15, 64
buying, 8, 14, 24, 49

C
capped interest rates, 23
cards *see* credit cards
cars, 24, 30
cash, 9, 37
cashback cards, 47
cash surrender value, 29
CCJ *see* county court judgments
charge cards, 32
charities, 47
cheques, 37
collateral, 23, 30
collection agencies, 18, 60
complaints, 55
conditions of use, 48
consolidation loans, 62–3
consumer protection, 49
corrections, credit files, 20, 51–3

costs, 15, 22, 36–7, 42–3
see also interest
counselling services, 58–9
county court judgments (CCJs), 16–17, 19, 21
credit cards, 7, 32–49
  benefits, 44–5
  consumer rights, 48–9
  costs, 36–7
  format, 34–5
  fraud, 48
  interest, 36, 40–3
  lost/stolen, 48, 53, 55
  protection, 48
  revolving credit, 22
  statements, 38–41
credit files, 16–21, 31, 51–3, 69
credit limit, 25, 32, 37, 40
credit ratio analysis, 57
credit reference agencies, 16–21, 51–3
creditors, 65, 68

D
daily periodic rate, 43
debit cards, 33
debt
  assessment, 13
  collectors, 61
  consolidating, 62–3
  excessive, 64–5
  management, 56–9
  repayment, 15
  unpaid, 19
Debt Management Plan, 59
defaults, 19, 23, 31
deposits, house purchase, 26
discharge, bankruptcy, 67
discretionary spending, 13
disputes, 19, 48, 50–1, 53, 65
due date, 11, 41

E
early redemption, 27
electoral roll, 16, 21
emergencies, 44, 53, 64
ending balance method, 41
endowment policies, 27
equity release schemes, 28
errors, credit files, 50–3

F
faulty goods, 48
fees *see* costs
first charge, 28
fixed interest rates, 23, 27
footprints, 19
fraud, 53, 55
  bankruptcy, 68
  credit applications, 12
  credit cards, 48
  debit cards, 33

G
garnishing, wages, 31
gearing, 29
gilts, 9
gold cards, 45
Government loans, 9
grace period, 42–3
guarantors, 23

H
hire purchase, 24
holograms, 34
home equity loans, 25, 28, 63
home ownership, 13
  see also mortgages
home shopping, 49
household expenses, 13, 14

I
impersonation, 53
income, 13, 26, 68
individual voluntary agreement (IVA), 16, 69
inflation, 9
insurance, 29, 44, 45
interest, 10–11, 40–3
interest rates, 9, 23
  asset-based loans, 25
  base rate, 8
  credit cards, 36
  discharged bankrupts, 69
  excessive, 54
interest-only mortgage, 27
internet shopping, 49
introductory rates, 36, 37
IVA *see* individual voluntary agreement

INDEX

J
joint credit, 31

L
late payments, 36, 37, 42–3
lenders, 8
  credit reference agencies, 18–19
  debt collection, 60
  negotiation, 65
  types, 24–5
leverage, 6, 28–9
life insurance, 29
line of credit, 25
litigation, 59
living expenses, 13, 68
loans, 7, 22–31
  asset-based, 25
  bonds, 9
  consolidation, 62–3
  costs, 22
  credit files, 18
  direct mail offers, 63
  history, 10–11
  on margin, 28
  mortgages, 14, 22, 24, 26–7, 28
  personal, 25
  secured, 24, 30–1, 63, 68
  students, 24
lost cards, 48, 53, 55

M
magnetic strip, 34, 35
management, debt, 56–9
margin loans, 28
marketing scams, 55
mediation, 59
minimum payment, 41
minimum purchases, 54
Mondex, 46
Monetary Policy Committee (MPC), 9
monthly expenses, 13, 68
mortgages, 14, 22, 24, 26–8
  see also home ownership
MPC *see* Monetary Policy Committee

N
negative items, credit files, 19, 20, 31, 59
Notice of Correction, 51
Notice of Disassociation, 51

O
obtaining credit, 12–13
official receiver, 67
overextension, 13, 57
overhead costs, 13

P
passwords, 53, 54
pawnbrokers, 25
payment plans, 23, 32–3, 65
payment protection, 45
penalties, 27
Personal Identification Number (PIN), 35, 49, 54
personal information, 17–18, 54, 55
personal loans, 25
PIN *see* Personal Identification Number
plaintiffs, 17
platinum cards, 45
previous balance method, 41
principal, 22
property, security, 24, 30–1
protection, 48, 49, 50–3
purchases, 8, 14, 24
  credit cards, 37
  protection, 49

R
receivers, 67
redemption, mortgages, 27
reference numbers, 38
refinancing, 64
repayments, 15, 27
repossession, 30–1
returned cheques, 37
revolving credit, 22, 32
reward cards, 47
risk, 11, 12, 19

S
scams, 55
searches, credit history, 21
second charge, 28
secured loans, 11, 24, 30–1, 63, 68
securities, 28
security, credit cards, 34, 35
signatures, 35
smart cards, 46
speciality cards, 46–7
stability, 12
standard variable rate (SVR), 26
statements, 38–41
stolen cards, 48, 53, 55
storing credit, 14
student loans, 24
SVR *see* standard variable rate

T
telephone transactions, 49, 55
terms and conditions, 45
theft, 48, 53, 55
trustworthiness, 6–7, 12–13, 68

U
unfair practices, 54–5
utilities, 14

V
variable interest rates, 23

W
wages, garnished, 31

ACKNOWLEDGMENTS

AUTHOR'S ACKNOWLEDGMENTS

Marc Robinson wishes to thank the most respected credit expert in the United States, Robert McKinley, for his significant and valuable contributions. Marc would like to dedicate this book to Zachary Robinson, and to Bert and Phoebe Robinson for all their patience and support.

PUBLISHER'S ACKNOWLEDGMENTS

Dorling Kindersley would like to give special thanks to Sarah Pennells for all her help and invaluable advice. The publisher would also like to thank everyone who generously lent props for the photoshoots, and to the following for their help and participation:

Editorial Stephanie Rubenstein; **Jacket Editor** Jane Oliver-Jedrzejak; **Design and Layout** Hedayat Sandjari; Isabel de Cordova; **Picture researchers** Mark Dennis, Sam Ruston; **Jacket Designer** John Dinsdale; **Consultants** Nick Clemente; Skeeter; **Indexer** Indexing Specialists; **Proofreader** Caroline Curtis; **Photography** Anthony Nex; **Photographers' assistants** Victor Boghassian; Stephanie Fowler; **Models** Zachary Robinson; Kara Rubenstein; Victor Boghassian; Stephanie Rubenstein; **Preflighting** Mark Schroeder; **Special thanks to** Teresa Clavasquin for her generous support and assistance.

AUTHORS' BIOGRAPHIES

Adam Shaw presents BBC1's daily financial programme *Working Lunch*. He is also the author of *Political Rhubarb* and co-author of *Money and How to Make More of It*. He has presented *Business Breakfast* and *Financial World Tonight*. He has also reported from Japan, USA, Canada, and France.

Marc Robinson is a founding director of LEAP (Latino Education Achievement Project), a non-profit organization dedicated to empowering Latinos to be more informed, confident, and active participants in the US. He is also co-founder of Internet-based moneytours.com, a personal finance resource for corporations, universities, credit unions, and other institutions interested in helping their constituents make intelligent decisions about their financial lives. He is the author of the KISS guide on Personal Finance. He wrote the original *The Wall Street Journal Guide to Understanding Money and Markets* and co-published a personal finance series with Time Life Books. He wrote a children's book about onomatopoeia in different languages, and has produced coffee table books for *The Wall Street Journal* to commemorate its 100th anniversary, and for NBC to commemorate its 75th anniversary. In his two decades in the financial services industry, Marc has provided marketing consulting to many top Wall Street firms. He is admitted to practise law in New York State.

PICTURE CREDITS

Key: *a* above, *b* bottom, *c* centre, *l* left, *r* right, *t* top
Corbis: Ariel Skelley 4c.

The information contained in this publication is general in nature and is not intended to provide advice, guidance, or expertise of any nature regarding financial or investment decisions. Neither Dorling Kindersley nor any of its authors or contributors make any representations or warranties with respect to the professional experience or credentials of the authors or contributors, or to the merits of the information or materials contained herein. The reader should consult independent financial advisers and investment professionals prior to making any decision or plan.